VIRGINIA
WOOLF

KILLING THE ANGEL
IN THE HOUSE:
SEVEN ESSAYS

PENGUIN BOOKS

PENGUIN BOOKS

Published by the Penguin Group. Penguin Books Ltd, 27 Wrights Lane, London W8 5TZ, England. Penguin Books USA Inc., 375 Hudson Street, New York, New York 10014, USA. Penguin Books Australia Ltd, Ringwood, Victoria, Australia Penguin Books Canada Ltd, 10 Alcorn Avenue, Toronto, Ontario, Canada M4V 3B2. Penguin Books (NZ) Ltd, 182–190 Wairau Road, Auckland 10, New Zealand   Penguin Books Ltd, Registered Offices: Harmondsworth, Middlesex, England · 'The Feminine Note in Fiction', 'Women Novelists', 'The Intellectual Status of Women', 'Two Women' and 'Memories of a Working Women's Guild' are taken from *A Woman's Essays* by Virginia Woolf, edited by Rachel Bowlby and published by Penguin Books in 1992. 'Professions for Women' and 'Ellen Terry' are taken from *The Crowded Dance of Modern Life* by Virginia Woolf, edited by Rachel Bowlby and published by Penguin Books in 1993. This edition published 1995   Selection, introduction and notes copyright © Rachel Bowlby, 1992, 1993   The moral right of the editor has been asserted   Typeset by Datix International Limited, Bungay, Suffolk. Printed in England by Clays Ltd, St Ives plc   ·

10 9 8 7 6 5 4 3 2 1

CONTENTS

Professions for Women

Virginia Woolf read this lecture to the National Society for Women's Service on 21 January 1931; it was published posthumously in *The Death of the Moth*, 1942

When your secretary[1] invited me to come here, she told me that your Society is concerned with the employment of women and she suggested that I might tell you something about my own professional experiences. It is true I am a woman; it is true I am employed; but what professional experiences have I had? It is difficult to say. My profession is literature; and in that profession there are fewer experiences for women than in any other, with the exception of the stage – fewer, I mean, that are peculiar to women. For the road was cut many years ago – by Fanny Burney, by Aphra Behn, by Harriet Martineau, by Jane Austen, by George Eliot[2] – many famous women, and many more unknown and forgotten, have been before me, making the path smooth, and regulating my steps. Thus, when I came to write, there were very few material obstacles in my way. Writing was a reputable and harmless occupation. The family peace was not broken by the scratching of a pen. No demand was made upon the family purse. For ten and sixpence one can buy paper enough to write all the plays of Shakespeare – if one has a mind that way. Pianos and models, Paris, Vienna and Berlin, masters and mistresses, are not needed by a writer. The cheapness of writing paper is, of course, the reason why women have succeeded as writers before they have succeeded in the other professions.

But to tell you my story – it is a simple one. You have only got to figure to yourselves a girl in a bedroom with a pen in her hand. She had only to move that pen from left to right – from ten o'clock to one. Then it occurred to her to do what is simple and cheap enough after all – to slip a few of those pages into an envelope, fix a penny stamp in the corner, and drop the envelope into the red box at the corner. It was thus that I became a journalist; and my effort was rewarded on the first day of the following month – a very glorious day it was for me – by a letter from an editor containing a cheque for one pound ten shillings and sixpence. But to show you how little I deserve to be called a professional woman, how little I know of the struggles and difficulties of such lives, I have to admit that instead of spending that sum upon bread and butter, rent, shoes and stockings, or butcher's bills, I went out and bought a cat – a beautiful cat, a Persian cat, which very soon involved me in bitter disputes with my neighbours.

What could be easier than to write articles and to buy Persian cats with the profits? But wait a moment. Articles have to be about something. Mine, I seem to remember, was about a novel by a famous man. And while I was writing this review, I discovered that if I were going to review books I should need to do battle with a certain phantom. And the phantom was a woman, and when I came to know her better I called her after the heroine of a famous poem, The Angel in the House.[3] It was she who used to come between me and my paper when I was writing reviews. It was she who bothered me and wasted my time and so tormented me that at last I killed her. You who come of a younger and happier generation may not have heard of her – you may not know what I mean by the Angel in the House. I will describe her as shortly as I can. She was intensely sympathetic. She was immensely charming. She was utterly unselfish. She excelled in the difficult arts of family life. She sacrificed herself daily. If there was chicken, she took the leg; if there was a draught she sat in it – in short she was so constituted that she never had a mind or a wish of her own, but preferred to sympathize always with the minds and wishes of others. Above all – I need not say it – she was pure. Her purity was supposed to be her chief beauty – her blushes, her great grace. In those days – the last of Queen Victoria – every house had its Angel. And when I came to write I encountered her with the very first words. The shadow of her wings fell on my page; I heard the rustling of her skirts in the room. Directly, that is to say, I took my pen

3

in my hand to review that novel by a famous man, she slipped behind me and whispered: 'My dear, you are a young woman. You are writing about a book that has been written by a man. Be sympathetic; be tender; flatter; deceive; use all the arts and wiles of our sex. Never let anybody guess that you have a mind of your own. Above all, be pure.' And she made as if to guide my pen. I now record the one act for which I take some credit to myself, though the credit rightly belongs to some excellent ancestors of mine who left me a certain sum of money – shall we say five hundred pounds a year? – so that it was not necessary for me to depend solely on charm for my living. I turned upon her and caught her by the throat. I did my best to kill her. My excuse, if I were to be had up in a court of law, would be that I acted in self-defence. Had I not killed her she would have killed me. She would have plucked the heart out of my writing. For, as I found, directly I put pen to paper, you cannot review even a novel without having a mind of your own, without expressing what you think to be the truth about human relations, morality, sex. And all these questions, according to the Angel of the House, cannot be dealt with freely and openly by women; they must charm, they must conciliate, they must - to put it bluntly – tell lies if they are to succeed. Thus, whenever I felt the shadow of her wing or the radiance of her halo upon my page, I took up the

4 inkpot and flung it at her. She died hard. Her fictitious

nature was of great assistance to her. It is far harder to kill a phantom than a reality. She was always creeping back when I thought I had despatched her. Though I flatter myself that I killed her in the end, the struggle was severe; it took much time that had better have been spent upon learning Greek grammar; or in roaming the world in search of adventures. But it was a real experience; it was an experience that was bound to befall all women writers at that time. Killing the Angel in the House was part of the occupation of a woman writer.

But to continue my story. The Angel was dead; what then remained? You may say that what remained was a simple and common object – a young woman in a bedroom with an inkpot. In other words, now that she had rid herself of falsehood, that young woman had only to be herself. Ah, but what is 'herself'? I mean, what is a woman? I assure you, I do not know. I do not believe that you know. I do not believe that anybody can know until she has expressed herself in all the arts and professions open to human skill. That indeed is one of the reasons why I have come here – out of respect for you, who are in process of showing us by your experiments what a woman is, who are in process of providing us, by your failures and successes, with that extremely important piece of information.

But to continue the story of my professional experiences. I made one pound ten and six by my first review; and I bought a Persian cat with the proceeds. Then I grew ambitious. A Persian cat is all very well. I said; but a Persian cat is not enough. I must have a motor car. And it was thus that I became a novelist – for it is a very strange thing that people will give you a motor car if you will tell them a story. It is a still stranger thing that there is nothing so delightful in the world as telling stories. It is far pleasanter than writing reviews of famous novels. And yet, if I am to obey your secretary and tell you my professional experiences as a novelist, I must tell you about a very strange experience that befell me as a novelist. And to understand it you must try first to imagine a novelist's state of mind. I hope I am not giving away professional secrets if I say that a novelist's chief desire is to be as unconscious as possible. He has to induce in himself a state of perpetual lethargy. He wants life to proceed with the utmost quiet and regularity. He wants to see the same faces, to read the same books, to do the same things day after day, month after month, while he is writing, so that nothing may break the illusion in which he is living – so that nothing may disturb or disquiet the mysterious nosings about, feelings round, darts, dashes and sudden discoveries of that very shy and illusive spirit, the imagination. I suspect that this state is the same both for men and women. Be that as it may, I want you to imagine me writing a novel in a state of trance. I want you

to figure to yourselves a girl sitting with a pen in her

hand, which for minutes, and indeed for hours, she never dips into the inkpot. The image that comes to my mind when I think of this girl is the image of a fisherman lying sunk in dreams on the verge of a deep lake with a rod held out over the water. She was letting her imagination sweep unchecked round every rock and cranny of the world that lies submerged in the depths of our unconscious being. Now came the experience, the experience that I believe to be far commoner with women writers than with men. The line raced through the girl's fingers.[4] Her imagination had rushed away. It had sought the pools, the depths, the dark places where the largest fish slumber. And then there was a smash. There was an explosion. There was foam and confusion. The imagination had dashed itself against something hard. The girl was roused from her dream. She was indeed in a state of the most acute and difficult distress. To speak without figure she had thought of something, something about the body, about the passions which it was unfitting for her as a woman to say. Men, her reason told her, would be shocked. The consciousness of what men will say of a woman who speaks the truth about her passions had roused her from her artist's state of uncon- sciousness. She could write no more. The trance was over. Her imagination could work no longer. This I believe to be a very common experience with women writers – they are impeded by the extreme conventionality of the other sex. For though men sensibly allow themselves great 7 freedom in these respects, I doubt that they realize or can control the extreme severity with which they condemn such freedom in women.

These then were two very genuine experiences of my own. These were two of the adventures of my professional life. The first – killing the Angel in the House – I think I solved. She died. But the second, telling the truth about my own experiences as a body, I do not think I solved. I doubt that any woman has solved it yet. The obstacles against her are still immensely powerful – and yet they are very difficult to define. Outwardly, what is simpler than to write books? Outwardly, what obstacles are there for a woman rather than for a man? Inwardly, I think, the case is very different; she has still many ghosts to fight, many prejudices to overcome. Indeed it will be a long time still, I think, before a woman can sit down to write a book without finding a phantom to be slain, a rock to be dashed against. And if this is so in literature, the freest of all professions for women, how is it in the new professions which you are now for the first time entering?

Those are the questions that I should like, had I time, to ask you. And indeed, if I have laid stress upon these professional experiences of mine, it is because I believe that they are, though in different forms, yours also. Even when the path is nominally open – when there is nothing to prevent a woman from being a doctor, a lawyer, a civil 8 servant – there are many phantoms and obstacles, as I believe, looming in her way. To discuss and define them is I think of great value and importance; for thus only can the labour be shared, the difficulties be solved. But besides this, it is necessary also to discuss the ends and the aims for which we are fighting, for which we are doing battle with these formidable obstacles. Those aims cannot be taken for granted; they must be perpetually questioned and examined. The whole position, as I see it – here in this hall surrounded by women practising for the first time in history I know not how many different professions – is one of extraordinary interest and importance. You have won rooms of your own in the house hitherto exclusively owned by men. You are able, though not without great labour and effort, to pay the rent. You are earning your five hundred pounds a year. But this freedom is only a beginning; the room is your own, but it is still bare. It has to be furnished; it has to be decorated; it has to be shared. How are you going to furnish it, how are you going to decorate it? With whom are you going to share it, and upon what terms? These, I think, are questions of the utmost importance and interest. For the first time in history you are able to ask them; for the first time you are able to decide for yourselves what the answers should be. Willingly would I stay and discuss those questions and answers – but not tonight. My time is up; and I must cease.

The Feminine Note in Fiction

A review of W. L. Courtney's *The Feminine Note in Fiction*
(Chapman and Hall, 1904), first published in the *Guardian*,
25 January 1905

Mr Courtney is certain that there is such a thing as the feminine note in fiction; he desires, moreover, to define its nature in the book before us, though at the start he admits that the feminine and masculine points of view are so different that it is difficult for one to understand the other. At any rate, he has made a laborious attempt; it is, perhaps, partly for the reason just stated that he ends where he begins. He gives us eight very patient and careful studies in the works of living women writers, in which he outlines the plots of their most successful books in detail. But we would have spared him the trouble willingly in exchange for some definite verdict; we can all read Mrs Humphry Ward,[1] for instance, and remember her story, but we want a critic to separate her virtues and her failings, to assign her right place in literature and to decide which of her characteristics are essentially feminine and why, and what is their significance. Mr Courtney implies by his title that he will, at any rate, accomplish this last, and it is with disappointment, though not with surprise, that we discover that he has done nothing of the kind. Is it not too soon after all to criticize the 'feminine note' in anything? and will not the adequate critic of women be a woman?

Mr Courtney, we think, feels something of this difficulty; his introduction, in which we expected to find some kind of summing-up, contains only some very tentative criticisms and conclusions. Women, we gather, are seldom artists, because they have a passion for details which conflicts with the proper artistic proportion of their work. We would cite Sappho and Jane Austen as examples of two great women who combine exquisite detail with a supreme sense of artistic proportion. Women, again, excel in 'close analytic miniature work'; they are more happy when they reproduce than when they create; their genius is for psychological analysis – all of which we note with interest, though we reserve our judgement for the next hundred years or bequeath the duty to our successor. Yet it is worth noting, as proof of the difficulty of the task which Mr Courtney has set himself, that he finds two at least of his eight women writers 'artists' – that two others possess a strength which in this age one has to call masculine, and, in fact, that no pair of them come under any one heading, though, of course, in the same way as men, they can be divided roughly into schools. At any rate, it seems to be clear according to Mr Courtney that more and more novels are written by women for women, which is the cause, he declares, that the novel as a work of art is disappearing. The first part of his statement may well be true; it means that women having found their voices have something to say which is naturally of supreme interest and meaning to women, but the value of which we cannot yet determine. The assertion that the woman novelist is extinguishing the novel as a work of art seems to us, however, more doubtful. It is, at any rate, possible that the widening of her intelligence by means of education and study of the Greek and Latin classics[2] may give her that sterner view of literature which will make an artist of her, so that, having blurted out her message somewhat formlessly, she will in due time fashion it into permanent artistic shape. Mr Courtney has given us material for many questions such as these, but his book has done nothing to prevent them from still remaining questions.

Women Novelists

A review of R. Brimley Johnson's *The Women Novelists* (Collins,
1918), first published in *The Times Literary Supplement*,
17 October 1918

By rights, or, more modestly, according to a theory of
ours, Mr Brimley Johnson should have written a book
amply calculated, according to the sex of the reader, to
cause gratification or annoyance, but of no value from a
critical point of view. Experience seems to prove that to
criticize the work of a sex as a sex is merely to state with
almost invariable acrimony prejudices derived from the
fact that you are either a man or a woman. By some lucky
balance of qualities Mr Brimley Johnson has delivered his
opinion of women novelists without this fatal bias, so that,
besides saying some very interesting things about literature, he says also many that are even more interesting
about the peculiar qualities of literature that is written by
women.

Given this unusual absence of partisanship, the interest
and also the complexity of the subject can scarcely be
over-stated. Mr Johnson, who has read more novels by
women than most of us have heard of, is very cautious –
more apt to suggest than to define, and much disposed to   13

qualify his conclusions. Thus, though this book is not a mere study of the women novelists, but an attempt to prove that they have followed a certain course of development, we should be puzzled to state what his theory amounts to. The question is one not merely of literature, but to a large extent of social history. What, for example, was the origin of the extraordinary outburst in the eighteenth century of novel writing by women? Why did it begin then, and not in the time of Elizabethan renaissance? Was the motive which finally determined them to write a desire to correct the current view of their sex expressed in so many volumes and for so many ages by male writers? If so, their art is at once possessed of an element which should be absent from the work of all previous writers. It is clear enough, however, that the work of Miss Burney, the mother of English fiction, was not inspired by any single wish to redress a grievance: the richness of the human scene as Dr Burney's daughter[1] had the chance of observing it provided a sufficient stimulus; but however strong the impulse to write had become, it had at the outset to meet opposition not only of circumstance but of opinion. Her first manuscripts were burnt by her step-mother's orders, and needlework was inflicted as a penance, much as, a few years later, Jane Austen would slip her writing beneath a book if anyone came in, and Charlotte Bronte stopped in the middle of her work to pare the potatoes. But the domestic problem, being overcome or compromised with, there remained the moral one. Miss Burney had showed that it was 'possible for a woman to write novels and be respectable', but the burden of proof still rested anew upon each authoress. Even so late as the mid-Victorian days George Eliot was accused of 'coarseness and immorality' in her attempt 'to familiarize the minds of our young women in the middle and higher ranks with matters on which their fathers and brothers would never venture to speak in their presence'

The effect of these repressions is still clearly to be traced in women's work, and the effect is wholly to the bad. The problem of art is sufficiently difficult in itself without having to respect the ignorance of young women's minds or to consider whether the public will think that the standard of moral purity displayed in your work is such as they have a right to expect from your sex. The attempt to conciliate, or more naturally to outrage, public opinion is equally a waste of energy and sin against art. It may have been not only with a view to obtaining impartial criticism that George Eliot and Miss Brontë adopted male pseudonyms[2] but in order to free their own consciousness as they wrote from the tyranny of what was expected from their sex. No more than men, however, could they free themselves from a more fundamental tyranny – the tyranny of sex itself. The effort to free themselves, or rather to enjoy what appears, perhaps erroneously, to be the comparative freedom of the male sex from that tyranny, is   15 another influence which has told disastrously upon the writing of women. When Mr Brimley Johnson says that 'imitation has not been, fortunately, the besetting sin of women novelists,' he has in mind no doubt the work of the exceptional women who imitated neither a sex nor any individual of either sex. But to take no more thought of their sex when they wrote than of the colour of their eyes was one of their conspicuous distinctions, and of itself a proof that they wrote at the bidding of a profound and imperious instinct. The women who wished to be taken for men in what they wrote were certainly common enough: and if they have given place to the women who wish to be taken for women the change is hardly for the better, since any emphasis, either of pride or of shame, laid consciously upon the sex of a writer is not only irritating but superfluous. As Mr Brimley Johnson again and again remarks, a woman's writing is always feminine; it cannot help being feminine; at its best it is most feminine: the only difficulty lies in defining what we mean by feminine. He shows his wisdom not only by advancing a great many suggestions, but also by accepting the fact, upsetting though it is, that women are apt to differ. Still, here are a few attempts: – 'Women are born preachers and always work for an ideal.' 'Woman is the moral realist, and her realism is not inspired by any ideal of art, but of sympathy with life.' For all her learning, 'George Eliot's outlook remains thoroughly emotional and feminine.' Women are humorous and satirical rather than imaginative. They have a greater sense of emotional purity than men, but a less alert sense of humour

No two people will accept without wishing to add to and qualify these attempts at a definition, and yet no one will admit that he can possibly mistake a novel written by a man for a novel written by a woman. There is the obvious and enormous difference of experience in the first place; but the essential difference lies in the fact not that men describe battles and women the birth of children, but that each sex describes itself. The first words in which either a man or a woman is described are generally enough to determine the sex of the writer; but though the absurdity of a woman's hero or a man's heroine is universally recognized, the sexes show themselves extremely quick at detecting each other's faults. No one can deny the authenticity of a Becky Sharp or of a Mr Woodhouse.[3] No doubt the desire and the capacity to criticize the other sex had its share in deciding women to write novels, for indeed that particular vein of comedy has been but slightly worked, and promises great richness. Then again, though men are the best judges of men and women of women, there is a side of each sex which is known only to the other, nor does this refer solely to the relationship of love. And finally (as regards this review at least) there rises for consideration the very difficult question of the difference between the man's and the woman's view of what constitutes the importance of any subject. From this spring not only marked differences of plot and incident, but infinite differences in selection, method, and style.

The Intellectual Status of Women

In the autumn of 1920 the successful
Edwardian novelist Arnold Bennett published a collection of
his essays, *Our Women: Chapters on the Sex-discord*. Woolf, staying
in the country and working on *Jacob's Room*, found herself
'making up a paper on women, as a counterblast
to Mr Bennett's adverse views reported in the papers'
(*Diary*, II, 26 Sept. 1920, p. 69). Bennett's assertion that
women were intellectually the inferior of men provoked Woolf
to think further about the issue, which she later explored in
A Room of One's Own (1929). On 2 October her friend
Desmond MacCarthy published the following review of
Bennett's book in the *New Statesman*, under
his pseudonym, Affable Hawk

*Samuel Butler used to say when asked what he thought about
women, 'I think what every sensible man thinks'; and when
pressed further he would add, 'Sensible men never tell'. This
was ominous and also characteristic; the crusty bachelor was
a strong strain in him. Mr Arnold Bennett has written a
book about women – not my women, you observe, which is a
title that would suit most other books written on the subject.
For though such books often profess to be results of detached
observation and to be about women in general, they usually
contain only notes about certain types familiar to the author.* 19

There seems an irresistible tendency to generalize on the topic. It seems difficult to make an observation about two or three women without at once turning it into a proposition about all women. I own I have done this myself and said many things which seemed to me clever and penetrating at the time, but were not scientific. One such aphorism I recall because the first half of it would meet, I think, with Mr Bennett's assent, since he quotes with approval Lady Mary Montagu's remark.¹ 'I have never in all my various travels seen but two sorts of people, and those very like one another; I mean, men and women.' My aphorism ran thus: 'Men and women are really more alike than they can believe each other to be; but they ought not to behave to each other as though this were true.'

Mr Bennett's book, unlike most books about women, is not an essay on love. It is a book about economics. The influence of the economic factor on feminine characteristics and on the relations between men and women is the main theme of his discourse. It is a sensible book and like many books which strike one immediately as sensible and straightforward, superficial. It is readable but not at all brilliant.

He lets one cat out of the bag – oddly enough, rather nervously. The cat in question I should have thought had been scampering about people's minds too long to make apologies necessary, but Mr Bennett is perhaps extra reluctant to let it loose because he is a convinced feminist. He finds it difficult to say, yet say it he does, that women are inferior to

20

men in intellectual power, especially in that kind of power which is described as creative. Certainly, that fact stares one in the face; and he admits that 'no amount of education and liberty of action will sensibly alter it.' 'The literature of the world can show at least fifty male poets greater than any woman poet . . .' (Yes, unless you believe with Samuel Butler that a woman wrote the Odyssey[2]) 'With the possible exception of Emily Bronte, no woman novelist has yet produced a novel to equal the great novels of men.' (On the whole that is true: assent is in this case a little more doubtful.) 'No woman at all has achieved either painting or sculpture that is better than second-rate, or music that is better than second-rate.' (True; remember the standard is the masterpieces of the world.) 'Nor has any woman come anywhere near the top in criticism.' (True.) 'Can anybody name a celebrated woman philosopher; or a woman who has made a first-rate scientific discovery; or a woman who has arrived at a first-rate generalization of any sort?' (No: I remember the standard again.) I cannot conceive anybody who considers facts impartially coming to any other conclusions. Though it is true that a small percentage of women are as clever as clever men, on the whole intellect is a masculine speciality. Some women undoubtedly have genius, but genius in a lesser degree than Shakespeare, Newton, Michael Angelo, Beethoven, Tolstoy. The average intellectual power of women also seems a good deal lower. If you tranferred the intellect of a clever but not remarkably clever man to a woman, you *would make her at once into a remarkably clever woman, and I expect the same is true of general organizing capacity: a feminine Ford[3] would be one of the world's wonders.*

And what then? Well, intellect means in the long run, and on the whole, domination.

It is indubitable that if women were a nation instead of a sex, their country would not be considered to have contributed much to the world's art of discoveries. Is this a very depressing conclusion for women? I do not see why it should be; we most of us have got used to the idea that we are not going to be Aristotles or Rembrandts, and are quite satisfied to be in the running for the sixth or seventh places, let alone the second or third which women have reached.

There is a passage worth drawing attention to on p. 105: 'I shall continue to assert,' says Mr Bennett, 'not only that even in this very advanced year women as a sex love to be dominated, but that for some thousands of years, if not for ever, they always will love to be dominated. This desire to be dominated is in itself a proof of intellectual inferiority. It is distinctive and survives, despite a general impression in certain quarters that recent progressive events have in some mysterious way put an end to it.' Well, men of inferior intellect do not wish to be dominated, and it is often very unfortunate that they do not. Therefore this desire which Mr Bennett attributes to women has nothing to do with intellectual inferiority. He says it is 'instinctive', but leaves it at that. This is an 22 *example of his superficial treatment of his subject.*

At the end of the book he gives an example of 'the sex-discord', that is to say the sort of way men and women misunderstand each other. The quarrel in this instance is over a gardener and some chrysanthemums. Jack and Jill fall out over this little matter, and as long as the quarrel lasts they think very badly of each other's character, Mr Bennett gets inside the head of each with great skill; but there is something queer about his version of matrimonial quarrels. I think what is wrong with it (I felt the same thing in These Twain[4]) is that his couples do not strike one as people who are really intimate. It may be true that most married people are not intimate. Intimacy is a gift, and implies a power of being expressive and, above all, caring for intimacy. Anyhow, the lack of it between Jack and Jill make them uninteresting, and his little sketch does not get down too deep.

About twelve years ago a book called Sex and Character, by Otto Weininger, was published, which created some stir. (Translation published by Heinemann.) It was written by a young Jew who committed suicide, and it is said that it had such a depressing effect on feminine readers that at least two of them followed his example. It was an honest, wild book, full of ingenious, highly questionable reasoning, insight and unfairness. It began with a general characterization of Woman, 'W', which was then divided into two main types, the Courtesan and the Mother, differentiated by their preoccupation with lovers or with children. It ended with discourse upon abnormal types of women and a definition of hysteria as   23 '*the organic mendacity of women*'. *In every human being there were mixed the two elements, 'M' (Man) and 'W' (Woman), just as these characteristics appear physiologically in each sex. To 'M' Weininger attributed all the admirable moral and intellectual qualities and to 'W' all the bad ones. Women therefore came out badly, for there was by hypothesis more 'W' in them than in the great majority of men.*

Another book on women has just appeared, The Good Englishwoman, *by Mr Orlo Williams. This is a collection of light, neatly written essays, of a friendly and soothing character. The author confines himself to the Englishwoman, and his book is more a study of manners and social habits than of sex. His address contains a good deal of flattery, but it is really more condescending. Mr Bennett is not condescending.*

Affable Hawk.

On 9 October the *New Statesman* printed the following letter from Woolf, followed by Affable Hawk's reply

To the Editor of the New Statesman.

Sir, – Like most women, I am unable to face the depression and the loss of self respect which Mr Arnold Bennett's blame and Mr Orlo Williams's praise – if it is not the other way about – would certainly cause me if I read their books in the bulk. I taste them, therefore, in sips at the hands of reviewers. But I cannot swallow the teaspoonful administered in your columns last week by Affable Hawk. The fact that women are inferior to men in intellectual power, he says, 'stares him in the face'. He goes on to agree with Mr Bennett's conclusion that 'no amount of education and liberty of action will sensibly alter it'. How, then, does Affable Hawk account for the fact which stares me, and I should have thought any other impartial observer, in the face, that the seventeenth century produced more remarkable women than the sixteenth, the eighteenth than the seventeenth, and the nineteenth than all three put together? When I compare the Duchess of Newcastle with Jane Austen, the matchless Orinda and Emily Brontë, Mrs Heywood with George Eliot, Aphra Behn with Charlotte Brontë, Jane Grey with Jane Harrison,[5] the advance in intellectual power seems to me not only sensible but immense; the comparison with men not in the least one that inclines me to suicide; and the effects of education and liberty scarcely to be over-rated. In short, though pessimism about the other sex is always delightful and invigorating, it seems a little sanguine of Mr Bennett and Affable Hawk to indulge in it with such certainty on the evidence before them. Thus, though women have every reason to hope that the intellect of the male sex is steadily diminishing, it would be unwise, until they have more evidence than the great war and the great peace supply, to announce it as a fact. In conclusion, if Affable Hawk sincerely wishes to discover a great poetess, 25 why does he let himself be fobbed off with a possible authoress of the *Odyssey*? Naturally, I cannot claim I know Greek as Mr Bennett and Affable Hawk know it, but I have often been told that Sappho was a woman, and that Plato and Aristotle placed her with Homer and Archilochus[6] among the greatest of their poets. That Mr Bennett can name fifty of the male sex who are indisputably her superiors is therefore a welcome surprise, and if he will publish their names I will promise, as an act of that submission which is so dear to my sex, not only to buy their works but, so far as my faculties allow, to learn them by heart. – Yours, etc.,

Virginia Woolf.

Affable Hawk writes: Sappho was at the height of her fame about 610 BC. She was a contemporary of Jeremiah and Nebuchadnezzar; when she wrote the Buddha was not born. This was a long time ago. Perhaps when Herculaneum[7] gives up its treasures her works will be found; at present we only possess two short odes and fragments preserved in quotation, or fragments of fragments stuck like the wings of flies in the solidified glue of ancient grammarians. Still, Sappho is a very great name. Whether she can be ranged among the fifty greatest poets of the 2,500 years which followed her leap from the Leucadian promontory is, in these circumstances, hard to decide. Perhaps, had other dialect poets, say Burns,[8] survived only in happy quotations, and been such themes for poetry in themselves as she, of whom it could be believed that she turned in falling into a swan, their reputations, too, might be as great. But 2,500 years is a long time to wait for a second poetess for whom that claim might even plausibly be made. Suppose Mr Bennett were to grant the point of Sappho, that long interval remains to be explained on another hypothesis than that the creative mind in fullest power seems to have been the property of few men. There was nothing else to prevent down the ages, so far as I can see, women who always played and sang and studied music producing as many musicians from among their number as men have done. Of the millions who led the contemplative religious life surely, otherwise, one or two might have equalled the achievements of Aquinas or Thomas à Kempis?[9] And when later painting was within their reach what great names can they show? If in the nineteenth century a woman had existed with the intellect of Mill, would she not have forced her way to the front as well as Harriet Martineau[10] did? Mill thought that Mrs Taylor was his superior in every respect; but no friend agreed with him. Newton was a small farmer's son, Herschel a member of a German band, Faraday a blacksmith's son, Laplace[11] the child of a poor peasant. Nothing will persuade me that if among their contemporaries a woman, more favourably placed than they, had shown the same instinctive intellectual passion and capacity, she could not have done their work. Granted the intellect and a garden of peas, and a monk may become a Mendel.[12] I maintain Mr Bennett's case is 27 strong. *Mrs Woolf asks how I account for the seventeenth century producing more remarkable women than the sixteenth, the eighteenth than the seventeenth, and the nineteenth than all three put together, if education is not the cause, and therefore the explanation also, of the smallness of women's achievement when education was withheld from most women. Of course it is education which has increased the number of remarkable women and the merit of their work, but the facts remain (1) that unfavourable in many respects as the conditions of women have been in the past, they have not been more unfavourable than many men possessing extraordinary intellectual powers have overcome; (2) that in directions to which those conditions were less unfavourable (literature, poetry, music and painting), they have hardly attained, with the possible exception of fiction, the highest achievements reached by men; (3) that, in spite of education, in pursuits requiring pure intellect they have not rivalled men. This does not imply, however, that a small percentage of women are not just as clever as any clever men, just as good artists, just as good correlators of facts, only that it seems that they fall short of the few men who are best of all.*

On 16 October the *New Statesman* published Woolf's response to Affable Hawk's rejoinder

To the Editor of the New Statesman.

Sir, – To begin with Sappho. We do not, as in the hypothetical case of Burns suggested by Affable Hawk, judge her merely by her fragments. We supplement our judgement by the opinions of those to whom her works were known in their entirety. It is true that she was born 2,500 years ago. According to Affable Hawk the fact that no poetess of her genius has appeared from 600 BC to the eighteenth century proves that during that time there were no poetesses of potential genius. It follows that the absence of poetesses of moderate merit during that period proves that there were no women writers of potential mediocrity. There was no Sappho; but also, until the seventeenth or eighteenth century, there was no Marie Corelli and no Mrs Barclay.[13]

To account for the complete lack not only of good women writers but also of bad women writers I can conceive no reason unless it be that there was some external restraint upon their powers. For Affable Hawk admits that there have always been women of second or third rate ability. Why, unless they were forcibly prohibited, did they not express these gifts in writing, music, or painting? The case of Sappho, though so remote, throws, I think, a little light upon the problem. I quote J. A. Symonds:[14]

Several circumstances contributed to aid the development of lyric poetry in Lesbos. The customs of the Aeolians permitted

29

more social and domestic freedom than was common in Greece. Aeolian women were not confined to the harem like Ionians, or subjected to the rigorous discipline of the Spartans. While mixing freely with male society, they were highly educated and accustomed to express their sentiments to an extent unknown elsewhere in history - until, indeed, the present time.

And now to skip from Sappho to Ethel Smyth.[15]

'There was nothing else [but intellectual inferiority] to prevent down the ages, so far as I can see, women who always played, sang and studied music, producing as many musicians from among their number as men have done,' says Affable Hawk. Was there nothing to prevent Ethel Smyth from going to Munich? Was there no opposition from her father? Did she find that the playing, singing and study of music which well-to-do families provided for their daughters were such as to fit them to become musicians? Yet Ethel Smyth was born in the nineteenth century. There are no great women painters, says Affable Hawk, though painting is now within their reach. It is within reach – if that is to say there is sufficient money after the sons have been educated to permit of paints and studios for the daughters and no family reason requiring their presence at home. Otherwise they must make a dash for it and disregard a species of torture more exquisitely painful, I believe, than any that man can imagine. And this is in the twentieth century. But, Affable Hawk argues, a great creative mind would triumph over obstacles such as these. Can he point to a single one of the great geniuses of history who has sprung from a people stinted of education and held in subjection, as for example the Irish or the Jews? It seems to me indisputable that the conditions which make it possible for Shakespeare to exist are that he shall have had predecessors in his art, shall make one of a group where art is freely discussed and practised, and shall himself have the utmost freedom of action and experience. Perhaps in Lesbos, but never since, have these conditions been the lot of women. Affable Hawk then names several men who have triumphed over poverty and ignorance. His first example is Isaac Newton. Newton was the son of a farmer; he was sent to a grammar school; he objected to working on the farm; an uncle, a clergyman, advised that he should be exempted and prepared for college; and at the age of nineteen he was sent to Trinity College, Cambridge. (See DNB.) Newton, that is to say, had to encounter about the same amount of opposition that the daughter of a country solicitor encounters who wishes to go to Newnham in the year 1920. But his discouragement is not increased by the works of Mr Bennett, Mr Orlo Williams and Affable Hawk.

Putting that aside, my point is that you will not get a big Newton until you have produced a considerable number of lesser Newtons. Affable Hawk will, I hope, not accuse me of cowardice if I do not take up your space 31 with an inquiry into the careers of Laplace, Faraday, and Herschel, nor compare the lives and achievements of Aquinas and St Theresa, nor decide whether it was Mill or his friends who was mistaken about Mrs Mill. The fact, as I think we shall agree, is that women from the earliest times to the present day have brought forth the entire population of the universe This occupation has taken much time and strength. It has also brought them into subjection to men, and incidentally – if that were to the point – bred in them some of the most lovable and admirable qualities of the race. My difference with Affable Hawk is not that he denies the present intellectual equality of men and women. It is that he, with Mr Bennett, asserts that the mind of woman is not sensibly affected by education and liberty; that it is incapable of the highest achievements; and that it must remain for ever in the condition in which it now is. I must repeat that the fact that women have improved (which Affable Hawk now seems to admit), shows that they might still improve; for I cannot see why a limit should be set to their improvement in the nineteenth century rather than in the one hundred and nineteenth. But it is not education only that is needed. It is that women should have liberty of experience; that they should differ from men without fear and express their differences openly (for I do not agree with Affable Hawk that men and women are alike); that all activity of the mind should be so encouraged that there will always be in existence a nucleus of women who think, invent, imagine, and create as freely as men do, and with as little fear of ridicule and condescension. These conditions, in my view of great importance, are impeded by such statements as those of Affable Hawk and Mr Bennett, for a man has still much greater facilities than a woman for making his views known and respected. Certainly I cannot doubt that if such opinions prevail in the future we shall remain in a condition of half-civilized barbarism. At least that is how I define an eternity of dominion on the one hand and of servility on the other. For the degradation of being a slave is only equalled by the degradation of being a master. - Yours, etc.,

Virginia Woolf

Affable Hawk writes: If the freedom and education of women is impeded by the expression of my views, I shall argue no more.

Two Women

This is a review of the *Letters of Lady Augusta Stanley* (ed. the Dean of Windsor and Hector Bolitho, Gerald Howe, 1927) and Lady Barbara Stephen's *Emily Davies and Girton College* (Constable, 1927), first published in the *Nation and Athenaeum*, 23 April 1927

Up to the beginning of the nineteenth century the distinguished woman had almost invariably been an aristocrat. It was the great lady who ruled and wrote letters and influenced the course of politics. From the huge middle class few women rose to eminence, nor has the drabness of their lot received the attention which has been bestowed upon the splendours of the great and the miseries of the poor. There they remain, even in the early part of the nineteenth century, a vast body, living, marrying, bearing children in dull obscurity until at last we begin to wonder whether there was something in their condition itself – in the age at which they married, the number of children they bore, the privacy they lacked, the incomes they had not, the conventions which stifled them, and the education they never received which so affected them that though the middle class is the great reservoir from which we draw our distinguished men it has thrown up singularly few women to set beside them.

The profound interest of Lady Stephen's life of Miss Emily Davies lies in the light it throws upon this dark and obscure chapter of human history. Miss Davies was born in the year 1830, of middle-class parents who could afford to educate their sons but not their daughters. Her education was, she supposed, much the same as that of other clergymen's daughters at that time. 'Do they go to school? No. Do they have governesses at home? No. They have lessons and get on as they can.' But if their positive education had stopped at a little Latin, a little history, a little housework, it would not so much have mattered. It was what may be called the negative education, that which decrees not what you may do but what you may not do, that cramped and stifled. 'Probably only women who have laboured under it can understand the weight of discouragement produced by being perpetually told that, as women, nothing much is ever expected of them . . Women who have lived in the atmosphere produced by such teaching know how it stifles and chills; how hard it is to work courageously through it.' Preachers and rulers of both sexes nevertheless formulated the creed and enforced it vigorously. Charlotte Yonge wrote: 'I have no hesitation in declaring my full belief in the inferiority of women, nor that she brought it upon herself.'[1] She reminded her sex of a painful incident with a snake in a garden which had settled their destiny, Miss Yonge said, for ever. The mention of Woman's Rights made Queen Victoria so 35

furious[2] that 'she cannot contain herself'. Mr Greg, under-
lining his words, wrote that 'the essentials of a woman's
being are *that they are supported by, and they minister to
men.*'[3] The only other occupation allowed them, indeed,
was to become a governess or a needlewoman, 'and both
these employments were naturally overstocked' If women
wanted to paint there was, up to the year 1858, only one
life class in London where they could learn. If they were
musical there was the inevitable piano, but the chief aim
was to produce a brilliant mechanical execution, and Trollope's picture of four girls[4] all in the same room playing
on four pianos all of them out of tune seems to have been,
as Trollope's pictures usually are, based on fact. Writing
was the most accessible of the arts, and write they did, but
their books were deeply influenced by the angle from
which they were forced to observe the world. Half occupied, always interrupted, with much leisure but little time
to themselves and no money of their own, these armies of
listless women were either driven to find solace and occupation in religion, or, if that failed, they took, as Miss
Nightingale said, 'to that perpetual day dreaming which is
so dangerous'.[5] Some indeed envied the working classes,
and Miss Martineau frankly hailed[6] the ruin of her family
with delight. 'I, who had been obliged to write before
breakfast, or in some private way, had henceforth liberty
to do my own work in my own way, for we had lost our
36 gentility.' But the time had come when there were occa-

sional exceptions both among parents and among daughters. Mr Leigh Smith, for example, allowed his daughter Barbara the same income that he gave his sons. She at once started a school of an advanced character. Miss Garrett became a doctor because her parents, though shocked and anxious, would be reconciled if she were a success. Miss Davies had a brother who sympathized and helped her in her determination to reform the education of women. With such encouragement the three young women started in the middle of the nineteenth century to lead the army of the unemployed in search of work. But the war of one sex upon the rights and possessions of the other is by no means a straightforward affair of attack and victory or defeat. Neither the means nor the end itself is clear-cut and recognized. There is the very potent weapon, for example, of feminine charm – what use were they to make of that? Miss Garrett said[7] she felt 'so mean in trying to come over the doctors by all kinds of little feminine dodges'. Mrs Gurney[8] admitted the difficulty, but pointed out that 'Miss Marsh's success among the navvies,'[9] had been mainly won by these means, which, for good or for bad, were certainly of immense weight. It was agreed therefore that charm was to be employed. Thus we have the curious spectacle, at once so diverting and so humiliating, of grave and busy women doing fancy work and playing croquet in order that the male eye might be gratified and deceived. 'Three lovely girls' were placed 37 conspicuously in the front row at a meeting, and Miss Garrett herself sat there looking 'exactly like one of the girls whose instinct it is to do what you tell them'. For the arguments that they had to meet by these devious means were in themselves extremely indefinite. There was a thing called 'the tender home-bloom of maidenliness' which must not be touched. There was chastity, of course, and her handmaidens innocence, sweetness, unselfishness, sympathy; all of which might suffer if women were allowed to learn Latin and Greek. The *Saturday Review*[10] gave cogent expression to what men feared for women and needed of women in the year 1864. The idea of submitting young ladies to local university examinations 'almost takes one's breath away', the writer said. If examined they must be, steps must be taken to see that 'learned men advanced in years' were the examiners, and that the presumably aged wives of these aged gentlemen should occupy 'a commanding position in the gallery'. Even so it would be 'next to impossible to persuade the world that a pretty first-class woman came by her honours fairly'. For the truth was, the reviewer wrote, that 'there is a strong and ineradicable male instinct that a learned, or even an accomplished young woman is the most intolerable monster in creation' It was against instincts and prejudices such as these, tough as roots but intangible as sea mist, that Miss Davies had to fight. Her days passed in a round of the

most diverse occupations. Besides the actual labour of

raising money and fighting prejudice she had to decide the most delicate moral questions which, directly victory was within sight, began to be posed by the students and their parents. A mother, for example, would only entrust her with her daughter's education on condition that she should come home 'as if nothing had happened', and not 'take to anything eccentric'. The students, on the other hand, bored with watching the Edinburgh express slip a carriage at Hitchin or rolling the lawn with a heavy iron roller, took to playing football, and then invited their teachers to see them act scenes from Shakespeare and Swinburne dressed in men's clothes. This, indeed, was a very serious matter; the great George Eliot was consulted; Mr Russell Gurney was consulted, and also Mr Tomkinson. They decided that it was unwomanly; Hamlet must be played in a skirt.

Miss Davies herself was decidedly austere. When money for the college flowed in she refused to spend it on luxuries. She wanted rooms – always more and more rooms to house those unhappy girls dreaming their youth away in indolence or picking up a little knowledge in the family sitting-room. 'Privacy was the one luxury Miss Davies desired for the student, and in her eyes it was not a luxury – she despised luxuries – but a necessity.' But one room to themselves was enough. She did not believe that they needed armchairs to sit in or pictures to look at. She herself lived austerely in lodgings till she was seventy-two, combative, argumentative, frankly preferring a labour meeting at Venice to the pictures and the palaces, consumed with an abstract passion for justice to women which burnt up trivial personalities and made her a little intolerant of social frivolities. Was it worth while, she once asked, in her admirable, caustic manner, after meeting Lady Augusta Stanley, to go among the aristocracy? 'I felt directly that if I went to Lady Stanley's again, I must get a new bonnet. And is it well to spend one's money in bonnets and flys instead of on instructive books?' she wondered. For Miss Davies perhaps was a little deficient in feminine charm.

That was a charge that nobody could bring against Lady Augusta Stanley. No two women could on the surface have less in common. Lady Augusta, it is true, was no more highly educated in a bookish sense than the middle-class women whom Miss Davies championed. But she was the finest flower of the education which for some centuries the little class of aristocratic women had enjoyed. She had been trained in her mother's drawing-room in Paris. She had talked to all the distinguished men and women of her time – Lamartine, Mérimée, Victor Hugo, the Duc de Broglie, Sainte-Beuve, Renan, Jenny Lind, Turgenev[11] – everybody came to talk to old Lady Elgin and to be entertained by her daughters. There she developed that abounding sensibility, that unquenchable sympathy which were to be so lavishly drawn upon in after years. For she was very young when she entered the Duchess of Kent's household. For fifteen years of her youth she lived there. For fifteen years she was the life and soul of that 'quiet affectionate dull household of old people at Frogmore and Clarence House' Nothing whatever happened. They drove out and she thought how charming the village children looked. They walked and the Duchess picked heather. They came home and the Duchess was tired. Yet not for a moment, pouring her heart out in profuse letters to her sisters, does she complain or wish for any other existence.

Seen through her peculiar magnifying glass, the slightest event in the life of the Royal family was either harrowing in the extreme or beyond words delightful. Prince Arthur was more handsome than ever. The Princess Helena was so lovely. Princess Ada fell from her pony. Prince Leo was naughty. The Beloved Duchess wanted a green umbrella. The measles had come out, but, alas, they threatened to go in again. One might suppose, to listen to Lady Augusta exclaiming and protesting in alternate rapture and despair, that to read aloud to the old Duchess of Kent was the most exciting of occupations, and that the old ladies' rheumatisms and headaches were catastrophes of the first order. For inevitably the power of sympathy when so highly developed and discharged solely upon personal relations tends to produce a hothouse atmosphere in which domestic details assume prodigious proportions and the mind feeds upon every detail of death and disease with a gluttonous relish. The space devoted in this volume to illness and marriage entirely outweighs any reference to art, literature or politics. It is all personal, emotional, and detailed as one of the novels which were written so inevitably by women.

It was such a life as this and such an atmosphere as this that Mr Greg and the *Saturday Review* and many men who had themselves enjoyed the utmost rigours of education wished to see preserved. And perhaps there was some excuse for them. It is difficult to be sure, after all, that a college don is the highest type of humanity known to us; and there is something in Lady Augusta's power to magnify the common and illumine the dull which seems to imply a very arduous education of some sort behind it. Nevertheless, as one studies the lives of the two women side by side, one cannot doubt that Miss Davies got more interest, more pleasure, and more use out of one month of her life than Lady Augusta out of a whole year of hers. Some inkling of the fact seems to have reached Lady Augusta even at Windsor Castle. Perhaps being a woman of the old type is a little exhausting; perhaps it is not altogether satisfying. Lady Augusta at any rate seems to have got wind of other possibilities. She liked the society of literary people best, she said. 'I had always said that I had wished to be a fellow of a college,' she added surprisingly. At any rate she was one of the first to support Miss

Davies in her demand for a university education for women. Did Miss Davies then sacrifice her book and buy her bonnet? Did the two women, so different in every other way, come together over this – the education of their sex? It is tempting to think so, and to imagine sprung from that union of the middle-class woman and the court lady some astonishing phoenix of the future who shall combine the new efficiency with the old amenity, the courage of the indomitable Miss Davies and Lady Augusta's charm.

Memories of a Working Women's Guild

This was written as an introduction to a volume entitled
Life As We Have Known It by Co-Operative Working Women
(ed. Margaret Llewellyn Davies, Hogarth Press, 1931). It was
first published, however, in the *Yale Review*, September
1930, with some differences that also appear in subsequent reprints
by Leonard Woolf, some of which are recorded in
the notes for their interest

When you asked me to write a preface to a book which
you had collected of papers by working women I replied
that I would be drowned rather than write a preface to
any book whatsoever. Books should stand on their own
feet, my argument was (and I think it is a sound one). If
they need shoring up by a preface here, an introduction
there, they have no more right to exist than a table that
needs a wad of paper under one leg in order to stand
steady. But you left me the papers, and, turning them
over, I saw that on this occasion the argument did not
apply; this book is not a book. Turning the pages, I began
to ask myself what is that book then, if it is not a book?
What quality has it? What ideas does it suggest? What old
arguments and memories does it rouse in me? And as all
this had nothing to do with an introduction or a preface,

but brought you to mind and certain pictures from the past, I stretched my hand for a sheet of notepaper and wrote the following letter addressed not to the public but to you.

You have forgotten (I wrote) a hot June morning in Newcastle[1] in the year 1913, or at least you will not remember what I remember, because you were otherwise engaged. Your attention was entirely absorbed by a green table, several sheets of paper, and a bell. Moreover you were frequently interrupted. There was a woman wearing something like a Lord Mayor's chain round her shoulders; she took her seat perhaps at your right; there were other women without ornament save fountain pens and despatch boxes – they sat perhaps at your left. Soon a row had been formed up there on the platform, with tables and inkstands and tumblers of water; while we, many hundreds of us, scraped and shuffled and filled the entire body of some vast municipal building beneath. The proceedings somehow opened. Perhaps an organ played. Perhaps songs were sung. Then the talking and the laughing suddenly subsided. A bell struck; a figure rose; a woman took her way from among us; she mounted a platform; she spoke for precisely five minutes; she descended. Directly she sat down another woman rose; mounted the platform; spoke for precisely five minutes and descended; then a third rose, then a fourth – and so it went on, speaker following speaker, one from the right, one from the left, one from 45 the middle, one from the background – each took her way to the stand, said what she had to say, and gave place to her successor. There was something military in the regularity of the proceeding. They were like marksmen, I thought, standing up in turn with rifle raised to aim at a target. Sometimes they missed, and there was a roar of laughter; sometimes they hit, and there was a roar of applause. But whether the particular shot hit or missed there was no doubt about the carefulness of the aim. There was no beating the bush;[2] there were no phrases of easy eloquence. The speaker made her way to the stand primed with her subject. Determination and resolution were stamped on her face. There was so much to be said between the strokes of the bell that she could not waste one second. The moment had come for which she had been waiting, perhaps for many months. The moment had come for which she had stored hat, shoes and dress – there was an air of discreet novelty about her clothing. But above all the moment had come when she was going to speak her mind, the mind of her constituency, the mind of the women who had sent her from Devonshire, perhaps, or Sussex, or some black mining village in Yorkshire to speak their mind for them in Newcastle.

It soon became obvious that the mind which lay spread over so wide a stretch of England was a vigorous mind working with great activity. It was thinking in June 1913 of the reform of the Divorce Laws; of the taxation of land values; of the Minimum Wage. It was concerned with the care of maternity; with the Trades Board Act; with the education of children over fourteen; it was unanimously of opinion that Adult Suffrage should become a Government measure – it was thinking in short about every sort of public question, and it was thinking constructively and pugnaciously. Accrington did not see eye to eye with Halifax, nor Middlesbrough with Plymouth. There was argument and opposition; resolutions were lost and amendments won. Hands shot up stiff as swords, or were pressed as stiffly to the side. Speaker followed speaker; the morning was cut up into precise lengths of five minutes by the bell.

Meanwhile – let me try after seventeen years to sum up the thoughts that passed through the minds of your guests, who had come from London and elsewhere, not to take part, but to listen – meanwhile what was it all about? What was the meaning of it? These women were demanding divorce, education, the vote – all good things. They were demanding higher wages and shorter hours – what could be more reasonable? And yet, though it was all so reasonable, much of it so forcible, some of it so humorous, a weight of discomfort was settling and shifting itself uneasily from side to side in your visitors' minds. All these questions – perhaps this was at the bottom of it – which matter so intensely to the people here, questions of sanitation and education and wages, this demand for an extra shilling, for another year at school, for eight hours instead of nine behind a counter or in a mill, leave me, in my own blood and bones, untouched. If every reform they demand was granted this very instant it would not touch one hair of my comfortable capitalistic head.[3] Hence my interest is merely altruistic. It is thin spread and moon coloured. There is no lifeblood or urgency about it. However hard I clap my hands or stamp my feet there is a hollowness in the sound which betrays me. I am a benevolent spectator. I am irretrievably cut off from the actors. I sit here hypocritically clapping and stamping, an outcast from the flock. On top of this too, my reason (it was in 1913, remember) could not help assuring me that even if the resolution, whatever it was, were carried unanimously the stamping and the clapping was an empty noise. It would pass out of the open window and become part of the clamour of the lorries and the striving of the hooves on the cobbles of Newcastle beneath – an inarticulate uproar. The mind might be active; the mind might be aggressive; but the mind was without a body; it had no legs or arms with which to enforce its will. In all that audience, among all those women who worked, who bore children, who scrubbed and cooked and bargained, there was not a single woman with a vote. Let them fire off their rifles if they liked, but they would hit no target; there were only blank cartridges inside. The thought was

irritating and depressing in the extreme.

The clock had now struck half-past eleven. Thus there were still then many hours to come. And if one had reached this stage of irritation and depression by half-past eleven in the morning, into what depths of boredom and despair would one not be plunged by half-past five in the evening? How could one sit out another day of speechifying? How could one, above all, face you, our hostess, with the information that your Congress had proved so insupportably exacerbating that one was going back to London by the very first train? The only chance lay in some happy conjuring trick, some change of attitude by which the mist and blankness of the speeches could be turned to blood and bone. Otherwise they remained intolerable. But suppose one played a childish game; suppose one said, as a child says, 'Let's pretend.' 'Let's pretend,' one said to oneself, looking at the speaker, 'that I am Mrs Giles of Durham City.' A woman of that name had just turned to address us. 'I am the wife of a miner. He comes back thick with grime. First he must have his bath. Then he must have his supper. But there is only a copper. My range is crowded with saucepans. There is no getting on with the work. All my crocks are covered with dust again. Why in the Lord's name have I not hot water and electric light laid on when middle-class women   . ' So up I jump and demand passionately 'labour saving appliances and housing reform'. Up I jump in the person of Mrs Giles of Durham; in the person of Mrs Phillips of Bacup; in the   49 person of Mrs Edwards of Wolverton. But after all the imagination is largely the child of the flesh. One could not be Mrs Giles of Durham because one's body had never stood at the wash-tub; one's hands had never wrung and scrubbed and chopped up whatever the meat may be that makes a miner's supper. The picture therefore was always letting in irrelevancies. One sat in an armchair or read a book. One saw landscapes and seascapes, perhaps Greece or Italy, where Mrs Giles or Mrs Edwards must have seen slag heaps and rows upon rows of slate-roofed houses. Something was always creeping in from a world that was not their world and making the picture false and the game too much of a game to be worth playing.

It was true that one could always correct these fancy portraits by taking a look at the actual person – at Mrs Thomas, or Mrs Langrish, or Miss Bolt of Hebden Bridge. They were worth looking at. Certainly, there were no armchairs, or electric light, or hot water laid on in their lives; no Greek hills or Mediterranean bays in their dreams. Bakers and butchers did not call for orders. They did not sign a cheque to pay the weekly bills, or order, over the telephone, a cheap but quite adequate seat at the Opera. If they travelled it was on excursion day, with food in string bags and babies[4] in their arms. They did not stroll through the house and say, that cover must go to the wash, or those sheets need changing. They plunged their arms in hot water and scrubbed the clothes themselves. In consequence their bodies were thick-set and muscular, their hands were large, and they had the slow emphatic gestures of people who are often stiff and fall tired in a heap on hard-backed chairs. They touched nothing lightly. They gripped papers and pencils as if they were brooms. Their faces were firm and heavily folded and lined with deep lines. It seemed as if their muscles were always taut and on the stretch. Their eyes looked as if they were always set on something actual – on saucepans that were boiling over, on children who were getting into mischief. Their lips never expressed the lighter and more detached emotions that come into play when the mind is perfectly at ease about the present. No, they were not in the least detached and easy and cosmopolitan. They were indigenous and rooted to one spot. Their very names were like the stones of the fields – common, grey, worn, obscure, docked of all splendours of association and romance. Of course they wanted baths and ovens and education and seventeen shillings instead of sixteen, and freedom and air and . . . 'And,' said Mrs Winthrop of Spennymoor, breaking into these thoughts with words that sounded like a refrain, 'we can wait.' . . . 'Yes,' she repeated, as if she had waited so long that the last lap of that immense vigil meant nothing for the end was in sight, 'we can wait.' And she got down rather stiffly from her perch and made her way back to her seat, an elderly woman dressed in her best clothes.

Then Mrs Potter spoke. Then Mrs Elphick. Then Mrs Holmes of Edgbaston. So it went on, and at last after innumerable speeches, after many communal meals at long tables and many arguments – the world was to be reformed, from top to bottom, in a variety of ways – after seeing Co-operative jams bottled and Co-operative biscuits made, after some song singing and ceremonies with banners, the new President received the chain of office with a kiss from the old President; the Congress dispersed; and the separate members who had stood up so valiantly and spoken out so boldly while the clock ticked its five minutes went back to Yorkshire and Wales and Sussex and Devonshire, and hung their clothes in the wardrobe and plunged their hands in the wash-tub again.

Later that summer the thoughts here so inadequately described, were again discussed, but not in a public hall hung with banners and loud with voices. The head office of the Guild, the centre from which speakers, papers, inkstands and tumblers, as I suppose, issued, was then in Hampstead. There, if I may remind you again of what you may well have forgotten, you invited us to come; you asked us to tell you how the Congress had impressed us. But I must pause on the threshold of that very dignified old house, with its eighteenth-century carvings and panelling, as we paused then in truth, for one could not enter and go upstairs without encountering Miss Kidd. Miss Kidd sat at her typewriter in the outer office. Miss Kidd, one felt, had set herself as a kind of watch-dog to ward off the meddlesome middle-class wasters of time who come prying into other people's business. Whether it was for this reason that she was dressed in a peculiar shade of deep purple I do not know. The colour seemed somehow symbolical. She was very short, but, owing to the weight which sat on her brow and the gloom which seemed to issue from her dress, she was also very heavy. An extra share of the world's grievances seemed to press upon her shoulders. When she clicked her typewriter one felt that she was making that instrument transmit messages of foreboding and ill-omen to an unheeding universe. But she relented, and like all relentings after gloom hers came with a sudden charm. Then we went upstairs, and upstairs we came upon a very different figure – upon Miss Lilian Harris,[5] indeed, who, whether it was due to her dress which was coffee coloured, or to her smile which was serene, or to the ash-tray in which many cigarettes had come amiably to an end,[6] seemed the image of detachment and equanimity. Had one not known that Miss Harris was to the Congress what the heart is to the remoter veins – that the great engine at Newcastle would not have thumped and throbbed without her – that she had collected and sorted and summoned and arranged that very intricate but orderly assembly of women – she would never have enlightened one. She had nothing whatever to do: she licked a few stamps and addressed a few envelopes

– it was a fad of hers – that was what her manner conveyed. It was Miss Harris who moved the papers off the chairs and got the tea-cups out of the cupboard. It was she who answered questions about figures and put her hand on the right file of letters infallibly and sat listening, without saying very much, but with calm comprehension, to whatever was said.

Again let me telescope into a few sentences, and into one scene, many random discussions on various occasions at various places. We said then – for you now emerged from an inner room, and if Miss Kidd was purple and Miss Harris was coffee coloured, you, speaking pictorially (and I dare not speak more explicitly) were kingfisher blue and as arrowy and decisive as that quick bird – we said then that the Congress had roused thoughts and ideas of the most diverse nature. It had been a revelation and a disillusionment. We had been humiliated and enraged. To begin with, all their talk, we said, or the greater part of it, was of matters of fact. They want baths and money.[7] To expect us, whose minds, such as they are, fly free at the end of a short length of capital to tie ourselves down again to that narrow plot of acquisitiveness and desire is impossible. We have baths and we have money. Therefore, however much we had sympathized our sympathy was largely fictitious. It was aesthetic sympathy, the sympathy of the eye and of the imagination, not of the heart and of the nerves; and such sympathy is always physically uncomfortable. Let us explain what we mean, we said. The Guild's women are magnificent to look at. Ladies in evening dress are lovelier far, but they lack the sculpturesque quality that these working women have. And though the range of expression is narrower in working women, their few expressions have a force and an emphasis, of tragedy or humour, which the faces of ladies lack. But, at the same time, it is much better to be a lady; ladies desire Mozart and Einstein[8] – that is, they desire things that are ends, not things that are means. Therefore to deride ladies and to imitate, as some of the speakers did, their mincing speech and little knowledge of what it pleases them to call 'reality' is, so it seems to us, not merely foolish but gives away the whole purpose of the Congress, for if it is better to be working women by all means let them remain so and not undergo the contamination which wealth and comfort bring. In spite of this, we went on, apart from prejudice and bandying compliments, undoubtedly the women at the Congress possess something which ladies lack, and something which is desirable, which is stimulating, and yet very difficult to define. One does not want to slip easily into fine phrases about 'contact with life', about 'facing facts' and 'the teaching of experience', for they invariably alienate the bearer, and moreover no working man or woman works harder or is in closer touch with reality than a painter with his brush or a writer with his pen.[9] But the quality that they have, judging from a phrase caught here and there, from a laugh, or a gesture seen in passing, is precisely the quality that Shakespeare would have enjoyed. One can fancy him slipping away from the brilliant salons of educated people to crack a joke in Mrs Robson's back kitchen. Indeed, we said, one of our most curious impressions at your Congress was that the 'poor', 'the working classes', or by whatever name you choose to call them, are not downtrodden, envious and exhausted; they are humorous and vigorous and thoroughly independent. Thus if it were possible to meet them not as masters or mistresses or customers with a counter between us, but over the wash-tub or in the parlour casually and congenially as fellow-beings with the same wishes and ends in view, a great liberation would follow, and perhaps friendship and sympathy would supervene. How many words must lurk in those women's vocabularies that have faded from ours! How many scenes must lie dormant in their eyes which are unseen by ours! What images and saws and proverbial sayings must still be current with them that have never reached the surface of print, and very likely they still keep the power which we have lost of making new ones. There were many shrewd sayings in the speeches at Congress which even the weight of a public meeting could not flatten out entirely But, we said, and here perhaps fiddled with a paper knife, or poked the fire impatiently by way of expressing our discontent, what is the use of it all? Our sympathy is fictitious, not real. Because the baker calls and we pay our bills with cheques, and our clothes are washed for us and we do not know the liver from the lights[10] we are condemned to remain forever shut up in the confines of the middle classes, wearing tail coats and silk stockings, and called Sir or Madam as the case may be, when we are all, in truth, simply Johns and Susans. And they remain equally deprived. For we have as much to give them as they to give us – wit and detachment, learning and poetry, and all those good gifts which those who have never answered bells or minded machines enjoy by right. But the barrier is impassable. And nothing perhaps exacerbated us more at the Congress (you must have noticed at times a certain irritability) than the thought that this force of theirs, this smouldering heat which broke the crust now and then and licked the surface with a hot and fearless flame, is about to break through and melt us together so that life will be richer and books more complex and society will pool its possessions instead of segregating them – all this is going to happen inevitably, thanks to you, very largely, and to Miss Harris and to Miss Kidd – but only when we are dead.

It was thus that we tried in the Guild Office that afternoon to explain the nature of fictitious sympathy and how it differs from real sympathy and how defective it is because it is not based upon sharing the same important emotions unconsciously. It was thus that we tried to describe the contradictory and complex feelings which beset the middle-class visitor when forced to sit out a Congress of working women in silence.

Perhaps it was at this point that you unlocked a drawer and took out a packet of papers. You did not at once untie the string that fastened them. Sometimes, you said, you got a letter which you could not bring yourself to burn: once or twice a Guildswoman had at your suggestion written a few pages about her life. It might be that we should find these papers interesting; that if we read them the women would cease to be symbols and would become instead individuals. But they were very fragmentary and ungrammatical; they had been jotted down in the intervals of housework. Indeed you could not at once bring yourself to give them up, as if to expose them to other eyes were a breach of confidence. It might be that their crudity[11] would only perplex, that the writing of people who do not know how to write – but at this point we burst in. In the first place, every Englishwoman knows how to write; in the second, even if she does not she has only to take her own life for subject and write the truth about that and not fiction or poetry for our interest to be so keenly roused that – that in short we cannot wait but must read the packet at once.

Thus pressed you did by degrees and with many delays – there was the war for example, and Miss Kidd died, and 58 you and Lilian Harris retired from the Guild, and a testimonial was given you in a casket, and many thousands of working women tried to say how you had changed their lives – tried to say what they will feel for you to their dying day – after all these interruptions you did at last gather the papers together and finally put them in my hands early this May. There they were, typed and docketed with a few snapshots and rather faded photographs stuck between the pages. And when at last I began to read, there started up in my mind's eye the figures that I had seen all those years ago at Newcastle with such bewilderment and curiosity. But they were no longer addressing a large meeting in Newcastle from a platform, dressed in their best clothes. The hot June day with its banners and its ceremonies had vanished, and instead one looked back into the past of the women who had stood there; into the four-roomed houses of miners, into the homes of small shopkeepers and agricultural labourers, into the fields and factories of fifty or sixty years ago. Mrs Burrows, for example, had worked in the Lincolnshire fens when she was eight with forty or fifty other children, and an old man had followed the gang with a long whip in his hand 'which he did not forget to use'. That was a strange reflection. Most of the women had started work at seven or eight, earning a penny on Saturday for washing a doorstep, or twopence a week for carrying suppers to the men at the iron foundry. They had gone into factories when they were fourteen. They had worked from seven in 59 the morning till eight or nine at night and had made thirteen or fifteen shillings a week. Out of this money they had saved some pence with which to buy their mother gin - she was often very tired in the evening and had borne perhaps thirteen children in as many years; or they fetched opium to assuage some miserable old woman's ague in the fens. Old Betty Rollett killed herself when she could get no more. They had seen half-starved women standing in rows to be paid for their match-boxes while they snuffed the roast meat of their employer's dinner cooking within. The smallpox had raged in Bethnal Green and they had known that the boxes went on being made in the sick-room and were sold to the public with the infection still thick on them. They had been so cold working in the wintry fields that they could not run when the ganger[12] gave them leave. They had waded through floods when the Wash overflowed its banks. Kind old ladies had given them parcels of food which had turned out to contain only crusts of bread and rancid bacon rind. All this they had done and seen and known when other children were still dabbling in seaside pools and spelling out fairy tales by the nursery fire. Naturally their faces had a different look on them. But they were, one remembered, firm faces, faces with something indomitable in their expression. Astonishing though it seems, human nature is so tough that it will take such wounds, even at the tenderest age, and 60 survive them. Keep a child mewed up in Bethnal Green and she will somehow snuff the country air from seeing the yellow dust on her brother's boots, and nothing will serve her but she must go there and see the 'clean ground', as she calls it, for herself. It was true that at first the 'bees were very frightening', but all the same she got to the country and the blue smoke and the cows came up to her expectation. Put girls, after a childhood of minding smaller brothers and washing doorsteps, into a factory when they are fourteen and their eyes will turn to the window and they will be happy because, as the workroom is six storeys high, the sun can be seen breaking over the hills, 'and that was always such a comfort and a help' Still stranger, if one needs additional proof of the strength of the human instinct to escape from bondage and attach itself whether to a country road or to a sunrise over the hills, is the fact that the highest ideals of duty flourish in an obscure hat factory as surely as on a battlefield. There were women in Christies' felt-hat factory, for example, who worked for 'honour'. They gave their lives to the cause of putting straight stitches into the bindings of men's hat brims. Felt is hard and thick; it is difficult to push the needle through; there are no rewards or glory to be won; but such is the incorrigible idealism of the human mind that there were 'trimmers' in those obscure places who would never put a crooked stitch in their work and ruthlessly tore out the crooked stitches of others. And as they drove in their straight stitches they reverenced Queen Victoria and thanked God, drawing up to the fire, that they were all married to good Conservative working men.

Certainly that story explained something of the force, of the obstinacy, which one had seen in the faces of the speakers at Newcastle. And then, if one went on reading these papers, one came upon other signs of the extraordinary vitality of the human spirit. That inborn energy which no amount of childbirth and washing up can quench had reached out, it seemed, and seized upon old copies of magazines; had attached itself to Dickens: had propped the poems of Burns against a dish cover to read while cooking. They read at meals; they read before going to the mill. They read Dickens and Scott and Henry George and Bulwer Lytton and Ella Wheeler Wilcox and Alice Meynell[13] and would like 'to get hold of any good history of the French Revolution, not Carlyle's, please',[14] and B. Russell on China,[15] and William Morris and Shelley and Florence Barclay and Samuel Butler's Notebooks – they read with the indiscriminate greed of a hungry appetite. that crams itself with toffee and beef and tarts and vinegar and champagne all in one gulp. Naturally such reading led to argument. The younger generation had the audacity to say that Queen Victoria was no better than an honest charwoman who had brought up her children respectably. They had the temerity to doubt whether to sew straight stitches into men's hat brims should be the sole aim and end of a woman's life. They started arguments and even held rudimentary debating societies on the floor of the factory In time the old trimmers even were shaken in their beliefs and came to think that there might be other ideals in the world besides straight stitches and Queen Victoria. Strange ideas indeed were seething in their brain. A girl, for instance, would reason, as she walked along the streets of a factory town, that she had no right to bring a child into the world if that child must earn its living in a mill. A chance saying in a book would fire her imagination to dream of future cities where there were to be baths and kitchens and washhouses and art galleries and museums and parks. The minds of working women were humming and their imaginations were awake. But how were they to realize their ideals? How were they to express their needs? It was hard enough for middle-class women with some amount of money and some degree of education behind them. But how could women whose hands were full of work, whose kitchens were thick with steam, who had neither education nor encouragement nor leisure remodel the world according to the ideas of working women? It was then, I suppose, sometime in the eighties, that the Women's Guild crept modestly and tentatively into existence. For a time it occupied an inch or two of space in the *Co-operative News* which called itself The Women's Corner It was there that Mrs Acland asked, 'Why should we not hold our Co-operative mothers' meetings, when we may bring our work and sit together, one of us reading some Co-operative work aloud, which may afterwards be discussed?' And on April 18th, 1883, she announced that the Women's Guild now numbered seven members. It was the Guild then that drew to itself all that restless wishing and dreaming. It was the Guild that made a central meeting place where formed and solidified all that was else so scattered and incoherent. The Guild must have given the older women, with their husbands and children, what 'clean ground' had given to the little girl in Bethnal Green, or the view of day breaking over the hills had given the girls in the hat factory. It gave them in the first place the rarest of all possessions – a room where they could sit down and think remote from boiling sauce-pans and crying children; and then that room became not merely a sitting-room and a meeting place, but a workshop where, laying their heads together, they could remodel their houses, could remodel their lives, could beat out this reform and that. And, as the membership grew, and twenty or thirty women made a practice of meeting weekly, so their ideas increased, and their interests widened. Instead of discussing merely their own taps and their own sinks and their own long hours and little pay, they began to discuss education and taxation and the conditions of work in the country at large. The women who had crept modestly in 1883 into Mrs Acland's sitting-room to sew and 'read some Co-operative work aloud', learnt to speak

64 out, boldly and authoritatively, about every question of

civic life. Thus it came about that Mrs Robson and Mrs Potter and Mrs Wright at Newcastle in 1913 were asking not only for baths and wages and electric light, but also for Adult Suffrage and the Taxation of Land Values and Divorce Law Reform. Thus in a year or two they were to demand peace and disarmament and the spread of Co-operative principles, not only among the working people of Great Britain, but among the nations of the world. And the force that lay behind their speeches and drove them home beyond the reach of eloquence was compact of many things – of men with whips, of sick-rooms where matchboxes were made, of hunger and cold, of many and difficult child-births, of much scrubbing and washing up, of reading Shelley and William Morris and Samuel Butler over the kitchen table, of weekly meetings of the Women's Guild, of Committees and Congresses at Manchester and elsewhere. And this lay behind the speeches of Mrs Robson and Mrs Potter and Mrs Wright. The papers which you sent me certainly threw some light upon the old curiosities and bewilderments which had made that Congress so memorable, and so thick with unanswered questions.

But that the pages here printed should mean all this to those who cannot supplement the written word with the memory of faces and the sound of voices is perhaps unlikely. It cannot be denied that the chapters here put together do not make a book – that as literature they have 65 many limitations. The writing, a literary critic might say, lacks detachment and imaginative breadth, even as the women themselves lacked variety and play of feature. Here are no reflections, he might object, no view of life as a whole, and no attempt to enter into the lives of other people. Poetry and fiction seem far beyond their horizon. Indeed, we are reminded of those obscure writers before the birth of Shakespeare who never travelled beyond the borders of their own parishes, who read no language but their own, and wrote with difficulty, finding few words and those awkwardly. And yet since writing is a complex art, much infected by life, these pages have some qualities even as literature that the literate and instructed might envy. Listen, for instance, to Mrs Scott, the felt-hat worker· 'I have been over the hill-tops when the snow drifts were over three feet high, and six feet in some places. I was in a blizzard in Hayfield and thought I should never get round the corners. But it was life on the moors; I seemed to know every blade of grass and where the flowers grew and all the little streams were my companions.' Could she have said that better if Oxford had made her a Doctor of Letters? Or take Mrs Layton's description of a match-box factory in Bethnal Green and how she looked through the fence and saw three ladies 'sitting in the shade doing some kind of fancy work'. It has something of the accuracy and clarity of a description by Defoe. And when Mrs Burrows brings to mind that bitter day when the children were about to eat their cold dinner and drink their cold tea under the hedge and the ugly woman asked them into her parlour saying, 'Bring these children into my house and let them eat their dinner there,' the words are simple, but it is difficult to see how they could say more. And then there is a fragment of a letter from Miss Kidd – the sombre purple figure who typed as if the weight of the world were on her shoulders. 'When I was a girl of seventeen,' she writes, 'my then employer, a gentleman of good position and high standing in the town, sent me to his home one night, ostensibly to take a parcel of books, but really with a very different object. When I arrived at the house all the family were away, and before he would allow me to leave he forced me to yield to him. At eighteen I was a mother.' Whether that is literature or not literature I do not presume to say, but that it explains much and reveals much is certain. Such then was the burden that rested on that sombre figure as she sat typing your letters, such were the memories she brooded as she guarded your door with her grim and indomitable fidelity.

But I will quote no more. These pages are only fragments. These voices are beginning only now to emerge from silence into half articulate speech. These lives are still half hidden in profound obscurity. To express even what is expressed here has been a work of labour and difficulty. The writing has been done in kitchens, at odds and ends of leisure, in the midst of distractions and 67 obstacles – but really there is no need for me, in a letter addressed to you, to lay stress upon the hardship of working women's lives. Have not you and Lilian Harris given your best years – but hush! you will not let me finish that sentence and therefore, with the old messages of friendship and admiration, I will make an end.

Ellen Terry

First published in the *New Statesman and Nation*,
8 February 1941

When she came on to the stage as Lady Cicely in *Captain Brassbound's Conversion*,[1] the stage collapsed like a house of cards and all the limelights were extinguished. When she spoke it was as if someone drew a bow over a ripe, richly seasoned cello; it grated, it glowed and it growled. Then she stopped speaking. She put on her glasses. She gazed intently at the back of a settee. She had forgotten her part. But did it matter? Speaking or silent, she was Lady Cicely – or was it Ellen Terry? At any rate, she filled the stage and all the other actors were put out, as electric lights are put out in the sun.

Yet this pause when she forgot what Lady Cicely said next was significant. It was a sign not that she was losing her memory and past her prime, as some said. It was a sign that Lady Cicely was not a part that suited her. Her son, Gordon Craig,[2] insists that she only forgot her part when there was something uncongenial in the words, when some speck of grit had got into the marvellous machine of her genius. When the part was congenial, when she was Shakespeare's Portia, Desdemona, Ophelia,[3] 69 every word, every comma was consumed. Even her eye-lashes acted. Her body lost its weight. Her son, a mere boy, could lift her in his arms. 'I am not myself,' she said 'Something comes upon me ... I am always-in-the-air, light and bodiless.' We, who can only remember her as Lady Cicely on the little stage at the Court Theatre, only remember what, compared with her Ophelia or her Portia, was as a picture postcard compared with the great Velasquez[4] in the gallery.

It is the fate of actors to leave only picture postcards behind them. Every night when the curtain goes down the beautiful coloured canvas is rubbed out. What remains is at best only a wavering, insubstantial phantom – a verbal life on the lips of the living. Ellen Terry was well aware of it. She tried herself, overcome by the greatness of Irving as Hamlet and indignant at the caricatures of his detractors, to describe what she remembered. It was in vain. She dropped her pen in despair. 'Oh God, that I were a writer!' she cried. 'Surely a *writer* could not string words together about Henry Irving's Hamlet and say *nothing, nothing*.' It never struck her, humble as she was, and obsessed by her lack of book learning, that she was, among other things, a writer. It never occurred to her when she wrote her autobiography, or scribbled page after page to Bernard Shaw late at night, dead tired after a rehearsal, that she was 'writing.'[5] The words in her beauti-

ful rapid hand bubbled off her pen. With dashes and

notes of exclamation she tried to give them the very tone
and stress of the spoken word. It is true, she could not
build a house with words, one room opening out of
another, and a staircase connecting the whole. But whatever she took up became in her warm, sensitive grasp a
tool. If it was a rolling-pin, she made perfect pastry. If it
was a carving knife, perfect slices fell from the leg of
mutton. If it were a pen, words peeled off, some broken,
some suspended in mid-air, but all far more expressive
than the tappings of the professional typewriter.[6]

With her pen then at odds and ends of time she has
painted a self-portrait. It is not an Academy portrait,[7]
glazed, framed, complete. It is rather a bundle of loose
leaves upon each of which she has dashed off a sketch for
a portrait – here a nose, here an arm, here a foot, and
there a mere scribble in the margin. The sketches done in
different moods, from different angles, sometimes contra-
dict each other. The nose cannot belong to the eyes; the
arm is out of all proportion to the foot. It is difficult to
assemble them. And there are blank pages, too. Some very
important features are left out. There was a self she did
not know, a gap she could not fill. Did she not take Walt
Whitman's words for a motto? 'Why, even I myself, I
often think, know little or nothing of my real life. Only a
few hints – a few diffused faint clues and indirections
I seek . . to trace out here?'[8]

Nevertheless, the first sketch is definite enough. It is

the sketch of her childhood. She was born to the stage. The stage was her cradle, her nursery. When other little girls were being taught sums and pot hooks she was being cuffed and buffeted into the practice of her profession. Her ears were boxed, her muscles suppled. All day she was hard at work on the boards. Late at night when other children were safe in bed she was stumbling along the dark streets wrapped in her father's cloak. And the dark street with its curtained windows was nothing but a sham to that little professional actress, and the rough-and-tumble life on the boards was her home, her reality. 'It's all such sham there,' she wrote – meaning by 'there' what she called 'life lived in houses' – 'sham – cold – hard – pretending. It's not sham here in our theatre – here all is real, warm and kind – we live a lovely spiritual life here.'

That is the first sketch. But turn to the next page. The child born to the stage has become a wife. She is married at sixteen to an elderly famous painter.[9] The theatre has gone; its lights are out and in its place is a quiet studio in a garden. In its place is a world full of pictures and 'gentle artistic people with quiet voices and elegant manners.' She sits mum in her corner while the famous elderly people talk over her head in quiet voices. She is content to wash her husband's brushes; to sit to him; to play her simple tunes on the piano to him while he paints. In the evening she wanders over the downs with the great poet, Tennyson. 'I was in Heaven,' she wrote. 'I never had one single pang of regret for the theatre.' If only it could have lasted! But somehow – here a blank page intervenes – she was an incongruous element in that quiet studio. She was too young, too vigorous, too vital, perhaps. At any rate, the marriage was a failure.

And so, skipping a page or two,[10] we come to the next sketch. She is a mother now. Two adorable children claim all her devotion. She is living in the depths of the country, in the heart of domesticity. She is up at six. She scrubs, she cooks, she sews. She teaches the children. She harnesses the pony. She fetches the milk. And again she is perfectly happy To live with children in a cottage, driving her little cart about the lanes, going to church on Sunday in blue and white cotton – that is the ideal life! She asks no more than that it shall go on like that for ever and ever. But one day the wheel comes off the pony cart. Huntsmen in pink leap over the hedge. One of them dismounts and offers help. He looks at the girl in a blue frock and exclaims: 'Good God! It's Nelly!' She looks at the huntsman in pink and cries, 'Charles Reade!'[11] And so, all in a jiffy, back she goes to the stage, and to forty pounds a week. For – that is the reason she gives – the bailiffs are in the house. She must make money.

At this point a very blank page confronts us. There is a gulf which we can only cross at a venture. Two sketches face each other; Ellen Terry in blue cotton among the hens; Ellen Terry robed and crowned as Lady Macbeth 73 on the stage of the Lyceum. The two sketches are contradictory yet they are both of the same woman. She hates the stage; yet she adores it. She worships her children; yet she forsakes them. She would like to live for ever among pigs and ducks in the open air; yet she spends the rest of her life among actors and actresses in the limelight. Her own attempt to explain the discrepancy is hardly convincing. 'I have always been more woman than artist,' she says. Irving put the theatre first. 'He had none of what I may call my bourgeois qualities – the love of being in love, the love of a home, the dislike of solitude.' She tries to persuade us that she was an ordinary woman enough; a better hand at pastry than most; an adept at keeping house; with an eye for colour, a taste for old furniture, and a positive passion for washing children's heads. If she went back to the stage it was because – well, what else could she do when the bailiffs were in the house?

This is the little sketch that she offers us to fill in the gap between the two Ellen Terrys – Ellen the mother, and Ellen the actress. But here we remember her warning: 'Why, even I myself know little or nothing of my real life.' There was something in her that she did not understand; something that came surging up from the depths and swept her away in its clutches. The voice she heard in the lane was not the voice of Charles Reade; nor was it the voice of the bailiffs. It was the voice of her genius; the urgent call of something that she could not define, could not suppress, and must obey. So she left her children and followed the voice back to the stage, back to the Lyceum, back to a long life of incessant toil, anguish and glory.

But, having gazed at the full-length portrait of Ellen Terry as Sargent[12] painted her, robed and crowned as Lady Macbeth, turn to the next page. It is done from another angle. Pen in hand, she is seated at her desk. A volume of Shakespeare lies before her. It is open at *Cymbeline*, and she is making careful notes in the margin. The part of Imogen presents great problems. She is, she says, 'on the rack' about her interpretation. Perhaps Bernard Shaw can throw light upon the question? A long letter from the brilliant young critic of the *Saturday Review*[13] lies beside Shakespeare. She has never met him, but for years they have written to each other, intimately, ardently, disputatiously, some of the best letters in the language. He says the most outrageous things. He compares dear Henry to an ogre, and Ellen to a captive chained in his cage. But Ellen Terry is quite capable of holding her own against Bernard Shaw. She scolds him, laughs at him, fondles him, and contradicts him. She has a curious sympathy for the advanced views that Henry Irving abominated. But what suggestions has the brilliant critic to make about Imogen? None apparently that she has not already thought for herself. She is as close and critical a student of Shakespeare as he is. She has studied every line, weighed the meaning of every word;

experimented with every gesture. Each of those golden moments when she becomes bodyless, not herself, is the result of months of minute and careful study. 'Art,' she quotes, 'needs that which we can give her, I assure you.'[14] In fact this mutable woman, all instinct, sympathy and sensation, is as painstaking a student, and as careful of the dignity of her art as Flaubert[15] himself.

But once more the expression on that serious face changes. She works like a slave – none harder. But she is quick to tell Mr Shaw that she does not work with her brain only. She is not in the least clever. Indeed, she is happy she tells him, *not to be clever*. She stresses the point with a jab of her pen. 'You clever people,' as she calls him and his friends, miss so much, mar so much. As for education, she never had a day's schooling in her life. As far as she can see, but the problem baffles her, the main spring of her art is imagination. Visit mad-houses, if you like; take notes; observe; study endlessly. But first, imagine. And so she takes her part away from the books out into the woods. Rambling down grassy rides, she lives her part until she is it. If a word jars or grates, she must re-think it, re-write it. Then when every phrase is her own, and every gesture spontaneous out she comes on to the stage and is Imogen, Ophelia, Desdemona.

But is she, even when the great moments are on her, a great actress? She doubts it. 'I cared more for love and life,' she says. Her face, too, has been no help to her. She cannot sustain emotion. Certainly she is not a great tragic actress. Now and again, perhaps, she has acted some comic part to perfection. But even while she analyses herself, as one artist to another, the sun slants upon an old kitchen chair. 'Thank the Lord for my eyes!' she exclaims. What a world of joy her eyes have brought her! Gazing at the old 'rush-bottomed, sturdy-legged, and wavy-backed' chair, the stage is gone, the limelights are out, the famous actress is forgotten.

Which, then, of all these women is the real Ellen Terry? How are we to put the scattered sketches together? Is she mother, wife, cook, critic, actress, or should she have been, after all, a painter? Each part seems the right part until she throws it aside and plays another. Something of Ellen Terry it seems overflowed every part and remained unacted. Shakespeare could not fit her; nor Ibsen; nor Shaw. The stage could not hold her; nor the nursery. But there is, after all, a greater dramatist than Shakespeare, Ibsen or Shaw. There is nature. Hers is so vast a stage, and so innumerable a company of actors, that for the most part she fobs them off with a tag or two. They come on and they go off without breaking the ranks. But now and again nature creates a new part, an original part. The actors who act that part always defy our attempts to name them. They will not act the stock parts – they forget the words, they improvise others of their own. But when they come on the stage falls like a pack of cards and the limelights are extinguished. That was Ellen Terry's fate – to act a new part. And thus while other actors are remembered because they were Hamlet, Phèdre or Cleopatra,[16] Ellen Terry is remembered because she was Ellen Terry.

Notes

PROFESSIONS FOR WOMEN

your secretary: i.e. Pippa (Philippa) Strachey (1872–1968). Writing this lecture gave Woolf the idea for the two major books that followed *The Waves*, as a diary entry for 20 January 1931 reveals:

I have this moment, while having my bath, conceived an entire new book – a sequel to a Room of One's Own – about the sexual life of women: to be called Professions for Women perhaps – Lord how exciting! This sprang out of my paper to be read on Wednesday to Pippa's society (*Diary*, IV, p. 6).

The books eventually became *The Years* (1937; Penguin Books, 1968; reprinted 1993) and *Three Guineas* (1938; Penguin Books, 1977; reprinted 1993). A diary entry for 23 January records that her lecture had been attended by 'Two hundred people; well dressed, keen, and often beautiful young women. Ethel [Smyth] in her blue kimono & wig' (*Diary*, IV, pp. 6–7). Vera Brittain wrote an account of it for the *New Statesman and Nation*, 31 January 1931, reprinted in *The Pargiters* (ed. Mitchell A. Leaska, Hogarth Press, 1978, p. xxxv), which also provides a much fuller text of this lecture, derived from a typescript in the Berg Collection, New York.

2. *Fanny Burney ... George Eliot*: Fanny Burney (1752–1840) was a novelist and diarist; Aphra Behn (1640–89), a poet, novelist and playwright, while Harriet Martineau (1802–76) wrote on a wide range of issues. Woolf had discussed women writers and the need to 'think back through our mothers' in *A Room of One's Own* (1929; Penguin Books, 1945; reprinted 1993, esp. p. 69).

3. *The Angel in the House*: a verse celebration of married love by Coventry Patmore (1823–96), idealizing women in the domestic role. A cancelled sentence in the longer version of the text defines her as 'the woman that men wished women to be' (*The Pargiters*, p. xxix).

4. *The line raced . . . fingers*: Woolf had described thinking as a process analogous to fishing in *A Room of One's Own* (1929; Penguin Books, 1993 edn, p. 5ff). In the longer version of the text the woman fishing is angrier at the repression of her forbidden thought. She is directed to wait 'until men have become so civilized that they are not shocked when a woman speaks the truth about her body' (*The Pargiters*, p. xl).

1. *Mrs Humphry Ward*: Victorian novelist philanthropist, (1851–1920), whose biography is reviewed in 'The Compromise', pp. 53ff.
2. *study of the Greek and Latin classics*: Woolf had herself been engaged in such studies from 1902, under the supervision of Janet Case. Middle-class girls' exclusion from this aspect of their brothers' education was a theme she often addressed, both explicitly and implicitly (for instance, in 'On Not Knowing Greek', pp. 93ff).

WOMAN NOVELISTS

1. *Dr Burney's daughter*: Fanny Burney's father was a musician.
2. *male pseudonyms*: Charlotte Brontë initially published under the name Currer Bell; George Eliot's real name was Marian Evans.
3. *a Becky Sharp ... a Mr Woodhouse*: characters in *Vanity Fair* (1848), by Thackeray, and *Emma* (1816), by Jane Austen.

1. *Lady Mary Montagu's remark*: in a letter to Lady Bute, 5 January 1748 (*The Complete Letters of Lady Mary Wortley Montagu*, 3 vols., ed. Robert Halsband, OUP, 1965–7, II, p. 392).

2. *Yes; unless you believe . . . a woman wrote the Odyssey*: in *The Authoress of the Odyssey* (1897), Samuel Butler had suggested that the epic had been written by a woman, arguing that it featured so many and such interesting women.

3. *Ford*: Henry Ford (1863–1947), the American industrialist and advocate of mass-production, founder of the Ford Motor Co. (1903).

4. *These Twain*: (1916) a novel by Arnold Bennett.

5. *When I compare the Duchess of Newcastle with . . . Jane Harrison*: Woolf drew up a similar list of women writers at the beginning of 'An Imperfect Lady'. The 'matchless Orinda' was the seventeenth-century poet Kathleen Philips (1631–64), thus described on her title pages; Eliza Heywood (1693–1756) was an actress, playwright and novelist; Aphra Behn (1640–89) was a prolific playwright, poet and novelist, and one of the first women to earn a living by writing; Jane Grey (1537–54), the great-granddaughter of Henry VII and queen for nine days, wrote letters and prayers; Jane Harrison (1850–1928) was a classical scholar whose

work on the representation of women in pre-classical Greece was much admired by Woolf.

6 *Archilochus*: the Greek satiric poet (714–676 BC).

7. *Herculaneum*: the Roman city buried under volcanic lava from nearby Vesuvius.

8. *Burns*: Robert Burns (1756–96), the Scottish dialect poet.

9. *Aquinas or Thomas à Kempis*: Thomas Aquinas (*c.* 1225–74) and Thomas à Kempis (*c.* 1380–1471) were both major religious thinkers of the Middle Ages.

10. *Harriet Martineau . . . Mrs Taylor*: Harriet Martineau (1801–76) was a well-known woman of letters. The Victorian philosopher John Stuart Mill thought Harriet Taylor (1808–59), later his wife, his intellectual superior. She was a strong advocate of women's rights, and it was under her influence that he wrote *The Subjection of Women* (1869), a substantial contribution to the subject.

11. *Herschel . . . Faraday . . . Laplace*: Sir William Herschel (1738–1822), a pioneering astronomer, discovered the planet Uranus and the moons of Saturn; Michael Faraday (1791–1867), a chemist and physicist, made important discoveries concerning electricity; Pierre Simon de Laplace (1745–1827) was an astronomer and mathematician who theorized about the creation of the universe.

12. *Mendel*: Gregor Mendel (1822–84) was an Austrian monk who formulated the laws of genetics.

13. *Marie Corelli . . Mrs Barclay*: Woolf's 'bad women writers' – Corelli (1855–1914) and Florence Barclay (1862–1921) – were authors of popular romances.

14. *J. A. Symonds*: from his *Studies of the Greek Poets* (2 vols., 3rd edn, 1893, I, p. 291).

15. *Ethel Smyth*: (1858–1944) a composer and committed feminist. Woolf had read her memoirs, *Impressions that Remained* (1919), the previous year (see *Diary*, I, 28 Nov. 1919, p. 315), though it was not until 1930 that the two women met and became friends.

TWO WOMEN

1. *I have no hesitation . herself*: from Charlotte Yonge's *Womankind* (1876).

2. *Queen Victoria so furious*: in Sir Theodore Martin's *Queen Victoria as I Knew Her* (1908).

3. *the essentials of . men*: the quotation is from Greg's 'Why are Women Redundant?', reprinted in *Literary and Social Judgements* (1868).

4. *Trollope's picture of four girls*: from *Miss Mackenzie* (1865).

5. *as Miss Nightingale said . . . dangerous*: Florence Nightingale as 'Cassandra' in her *Suggestions for Thought to the Searchers After Truth* (1860).

6. *Miss Martineau frankly hailed*: in her *Autobiography* (1877).

7. *Miss Garrett said*: in a letter to Emily Davies, 12 April 1862.

8. *Mrs Gurney*: supporter of the Girls' Public Day School Company, a scheme for the setting up of secondary schools for girls.

9. *navvies*: Catherine Marsh did some work with railway navvies, but came into her own distributing religious literature and lessons among the navvies constructing the Crystal Palace for the Great Exhibition of 1851. Her book *English Hearts and English Hands* (1858) was very popular.

10. *Saturday Review*: the article, entitled 'Feminine Wranglers', appeared on 23 July 1864.

11. *Lamartine ... Turgenev*: Alphonse de Lamartine (1790–1869), the French poet, writer and politician; Prosper Mérimée (1803–70), French novelist and short-story writer, the author of *Carmen* (1845); Victor Hugo (1802–85), the leading French romantic poet, novelist and dramatist; Duc de Broglie (1821–1901), the French statesman and man of letters; Charles Sainte-Beuve (1804–69), the French literary critic, admired by Matthew Arnold and others as the founder of modern criticism; Ernest Renan (1823–92), the writer, philosopher and Professor of Hebrew who applied scientific historical investigation to Christianity in

his *Vie de Jésus* (1863); Jenny Lind (1820–87), the Swedish-born soprano, nicknamed the 'Swedish Nightingale'; and Ivan Turgenev (1818–83), the Russian novelist and playwright much admired by Woolf.

MEMORIES OF A WORKING WOMEN'S GUILD

1. *a hot June morning in Newcastle*: changed in the other versions to Manchester, as though to fictionalize the proceedings (and Devonshire becomes Cornwall throughout). In a letter to Violet Dickinson sent from Sussex before the conference, Woolf had written: 'We're down here, but come up [to London] for a few days, and then retire to New Castle on Tyne to join the Cooperative Women' (*Letters*, II, late May 1913, p. 28).

2. *beating the bush*: in other editions, the more common phrase 'beating *about* the bush' was substituted. However, the original more clearly continues the shooting metaphor: 'beaters' were employed to scare birds into flight; here it is the women that are doing the shooting.

3. *my comfortable capitalistic head*: this strong phrase was subsequently diluted to become, 'it would not matter to me a single jot'

4. *babies*: more specifically described as 'hot' babies in later versions of the text.

5. *Miss Kidd ... Miss Lilian Harris*: these actual names were later changed to Miss Wick and Miss Janet Erskine.

6. *the ash-tray in which many cigarettes had come amiably to an end*: elsewhere, 'Miss Erskine may have been smoking a pipe – there was one on the table.' And further, 'She may have been reading a detective story – there was a book of that kind on the table.'

7. *They want baths and money*: the other versions included the following sentence: 'When people get together communally they always talk about baths and money: they always show the least desirable of their characteristics – their lust for conquest and their desire for possessions.'

8. *Einstein*: the scientist is elsewhere replaced by 'Cézanne and Shakespeare'.

9. *no working man or woman ... or a writer with his pen*: Woolf is crossing a line, or not thinking twice, in making her habitual analogy of writing and painting to crafts into a direct comparison with paid labour, skilled and unskilled.

10. *lights*: the lungs of beasts sold cheaply by butchers, often as pet food.

11. *crudity*: in the other versions, 'illiteracy'.

12. *the ganger*: a work overseer.

13. *They read Dickens and Scott ... Alice Meynell*: the absence of first names marks the first two out as

classics in comparison with the other names on the list; but they, like Henry George and the rest, were in every sense popular writers in the nineteenth century.

14. *not Carlyle's please*: Carlyle's *The French Revolution: A History* was published in three volumes in 1837.

15. *B. Russell on China*: Bertrand Russell's *The Problem of China* was published in 1922.

ELLEN TERRY

1. *Captain Brassbound's Conversion*: (1900) written by George Bernard Shaw for Ellen Terry (1847–1928); she performed as Lady Cicely in 1906, 1907 and 1908. Woolf wrote this essay in late November and early December 1940 for the New York *Harper's Bazaar*, prompted by interest in the subject (she had first written of Ellen Terry in her comedy *Freshwater* (ed. L. P. Ruotolo, 1976)), but also with some misgiving: 'I'm not sure of my audience in Harper's' – and later, 'Exhausted with the long struggle of writing 2,000 about Ellen Terry.' In the event, it was turned down by *Harper's* (26 January 1941) and appeared in the *New Statesman and Nation*, 8 February 1941 (*Diary*, V, pp. 330, 342, 343, 354).

2. *Her son, Gordon Craig*: author of *Ellen Terry and her Secret Self* (1931), and editor with C. St John of her

posthumous *Memoirs* (1933), both books read by Woolf in preparing this article (*Diary*, V, p. 342, note 17).

3. *Portia, Desdemona, Ophelia*: heroines in Shakespeare's *The Merchant of Venice, Othello* and *Hamlet*. From 1878 to 1902, Ellen Terry worked with Henry Irving, the greatest Shakespearian actor of his day.

4. *Velasquez, Diego Rodriguez de Silva y*: Spanish court painter (1599–1660) whose portraits were often life size or even larger.

5. *she was 'writing'*: Terry wrote *The Story of My Life* (1908, 2nd ed. 1922) and her correspondence with Shaw was published posthumously, edited by C. St John (1931).

6. *typewriter*: here, the typist, rather than the machine.

7. *not an Academy portrait*: for Woolf's views on Royal Academy taste, see 'The Royal Academy' (p. 13ff).

8. *Why, even I myself . . . trace out here*: from Whitman's 'When I Read the Book' (1847); used as an epigraph in her autobiography.

9. *an elderly famous painter*: George Frederic Watts (1817–1904); Ellen Terry was thirty years younger than Watts when she married him in 1864. Woolf's comedy *Freshwater* (ed. L. P. Ruotolo, 1976) is set on the Isle of Wight at the house of her great-aunt, Julia Margaret Cameron: it includes Tennyson, Watts, Ellen Terry and her young lover, John Craig, as characters.

10. *skipping a page or two*: during which Terry eloped with the architect Edward Godwin, and returned to the stage briefly in 1867 before leading a pastoral life in Harpenden, Hertfordshire.

11. *Charles Reade*: a popular Victorian novelist (1814–84).

12. *Sargent*: see note 7 on 'The Royal Academy', p. 186.

13. *Saturday Review*: George Bernard Shaw worked for this paper from 1895.

14. *I assure you*: the words of the actress Anne Oldfield (1683–1730), quoted by Terry in her autobiography.

15. *Flaubert*: the French novelist Gustave Flaubert (1821–1880) was totally committed to the craft of writing.

16. *Phèdre or Cleopatra*: the heroines of plays by Racine and Shakespeare.

For complete information about books available from Penguin and how to order them, please write to us at the appropriate address below. Please note that for copyright reasons the selection of books varies from country to country.

IN THE UNITED KINGDOM: Please write to *Dept. JC, Penguin Books Ltd, FREEPOST, West Drayton, Middlesex UB7 0BR.*

If you have any difficulty in obtaining a title, please send your order with the correct money, plus ten per cent for postage and packaging, to *PO Box No. 11, West Drayton, Middlesex UB7 0BR.*

IN THE UNITED STATES: Please write to *Consumer Sales, Penguin USA, P.O. Box 999, Dept. 17109, Bergenfield, New Jersey 07621-0120.* VISA and MasterCard holders call 1-800-253-6476 to order all Penguin titles.

IN CANADA: Please write to *Penguin Books Canada Ltd, 10 Alcorn Avenue, Suite 300, Toronto, Ontario M4V 3B2.*

IN AUSTRALIA: Please write to *Penguin Books Australia Ltd, P.O. Box 257, Ringwood, Victoria 3134.*

IN NEW ZEALAND: Please write to *Penguin Books (NZ) Ltd, Private Bag 102902, North Shore Mail Centre, Auckland 10.*

IN INDIA: Please write to *Penguin Books India Pvt Ltd, 706 Eros Apartments, 56 Nehru Place, New Delhi 110 019.*

IN THE NETHERLANDS: Please write to *Penguin Books Netherlands bv, Postbus 3507, NL-1001 AH Amsterdam.*

IN GERMANY: Please write to *Penguin Books Deutschland GmbH, Metzlerstrasse 26, 60594 Frankfurt am Main.*

IN SPAIN: Please write to *Penguin Books S. A., Bravo Murillo 19, 1o B, 28015 Madrid.*

IN ITALY: Please write to *Penguin Italia s.r.l., Via Felice Casati 20, I-20124 Milano.*

IN FRANCE: Please write to *Penguin France S. A., 17 rue Lejeune, F-31000 Toulouse.*

IN JAPAN: Please write to *Penguin Books Japan, Ishikiribashi Building, 2-5-4, Suido, Bunkyo-ku, Tokyo 112.*

IN GREECE: Please write to *Penguin Hellas Ltd, Dimocritou 3, GR-106 71 Athens.*

IN SOUTH AFRICA: Please write to *Longman Penguin Southern Africa (Pty) Ltd, Private Bag X08, Bertsham 2013.*